# Fear and Anxiety

# CAUSES & EFFECTS OF EMOTIONS

# CAUSES & EFFECTS OF EMOTIONS

# Fear and Anxiety

### Kim Etingoff

Mason Crest

Mason Crest
450 Parkway Drive, Suite D
Broomall, PA 19008
www.masoncrest.com

Printed and bound in the United States of America.

First printing
9 8 7 6 5 4 3 2 1

Series ISBN: 978-1-4222-3067-1
ISBN: 978-1-4222-3073-2
ebook ISBN: 978-1-4222-8766-8

The Library of Congress has cataloged the
hardcopy format(s) as follows:
          Library of Congress Cataloging-in-Publication Data

Etingoff, Kim.
  Fear and anxiety / Kim Etingoff.
      pages cm. — (Causes & effects of emotions)
  Audience: Grade 7 to 8.
  Includes index.
  ISBN 978-1-4222-3073-2 (hardback) — ISBN 978-1-4222-3067-1 (series) — ISBN 978-1-4222-8766-8 (ebook)  1. Fear—Juvenile literature. 2. Anxiety—Juvenile literature.  I. Title.
  BF575.F2E85 2014
  152.4'6—dc23
                                        2014004381

# CONTENTS

**KEY ICONS TO LOOK FOR:**

**Text-Dependent Questions:** These questions send the reader back to the text for more careful attention to the evidence presented there.

**Words to Understand:** These words with their easy-to-understand definitions will increase the reader's understanding of the text, while building vocabulary skills.

**Series Glossary of Key Terms:** This back-of-the book glossary contains terminology used throughout this series. Words found here increase the reader's ability to read and comprehend higher-level books and articles in this field.

**Research Projects:** Readers are pointed toward areas of further inquiry connected to each chapter. Suggestions are provided for projects that encourage deeper research and analysis.

**Sidebars:** This boxed material within the main text allows readers to build knowledge, gain insights, explore possibilities, and broaden their perspectives by weaving together additional information to provide realistic and holistic perspectives.

# INTRODUCTION

The journey of self-discovery for young adults can be a passage that includes times of introspection as well joyful experiences. It can also be a complicated route filled with confusing road signs and hazards along the way. The choices teens make will have lifelong impacts. From early romantic relationships to complex feelings of anxiousness, loneliness, and compassion, this series of books is designed specifically for young adults, tackling many of the challenges facing them as they navigate the social and emotional world around and within them. Each chapter explores the social emotional pitfalls and triumphs of young adults, using stories in which readers will see themselves reflected.

Adolescents encounter compound issues today in home, school, and community. Many young adults may feel ill equipped to identify and manage the broad range of emotions they experience as their minds and bodies change and grow. They face many adult problems without the knowledge and tools needed to find satisfactory solutions. Where do they fit in? Why are they afraid? Do others feel as lonely and lost as they do? How do they handle the emotions that can engulf them when a friend betrays them or they fail to make the grade? These are all important questions that young adults may face. Young adults need guidance to pilot their way through changing feelings that are influenced by peers, family relationships, and an ever-changing world. They need to know that they share common strengths and pressures with their peers. Realizing they are not alone with their questions can help them develop important attributes of resilience and hope.

The books in this series skillfully capture young people's everyday, real-life emotional journeys and provides practical and meaningful information that can offer hope to all who read them.

It covers topics that teens may be hesitant to discuss with others, giving them a context for their own feelings and relationships. It is an essential tool to help young adults understand themselves and their place in the world around them—and a valuable asset for teachers and counselors working to help young people become healthy, confident, and compassionate members of our society.

**Cindy Croft, M.A.Ed**
Director of the Center for Inclusive Child Care at Concordia University

# Words to Understand

**apprehension:** Worry or fear about the future.
**threaten:** Put in danger.
**potentially:** Able to become something in the future.

# ONE

## WHAT ARE FEAR
## AND ANXIETY?

Mya woke up suddenly, even before her alarm went off. She looked at the clock—6:58 in the morning. For a minute, she couldn't put all her thoughts together. Then they all came into clear, horrible focus.

Today was the day of Mya's big soccer match. Her team was in the finals, and they were set to play one of the best teams in the league. If they won this game, Mya's team would win the championship. Today was a big day.

As soon as Mya remembered the game, the vague, uneasy feeling she woke up with changed into a huge pit of pain in her stomach. Maybe she could just stay in bed and say she was sick, Mya thought.

But she forced herself out of bed. She was a forward player, so her job was to score goals. If she didn't score goals, then her

# Stress Meter

**Panic Attack!**

**Anxiety**

**Stressed**

**Coping**

**Relaxed**

Stress and anxiety often go hand-in-hand, with each making the other emotion seem worse.

The pressure to play well at a big game is one of the things that might make you feel anxious.

team might not win, and everyone would be disappointed. She had to play—but she had been feeling awful for days whenever she thought about the game.

This season, Mya had worked really hard to become a good soccer player. Her family was always pressuring her to be the star player. Her older brother had been an amazing player when he was in school, and the rest of her family wanted Mya to follow in her brother's footsteps. They made her go to extra practices, and whenever her brother came home, he would give Mya endless tips about playing well.

Mya's coach also put a lot of pressure on her. As Mya got better and better, the coach pushed her harder and harder. Whenever she missed a goal or showed up to practice a little late, the coach yelled at her. Now all of her teammates were counting on her to score goals too, because she had played so well this year.

The championship game was a little different from a regular

Feelings of anxiety affect the rest of our bodies as well. A stomachache is a common response to anxiety.

Knowing we'll have an audience for our performance is a factor that often heightens anxiety.

game, though. Only a few people watched most of Mya's games, mostly parents and friends. There would be hundreds of people at the championship game, some of them traveling from out of town. All of them would be watching Mya and her teammates win—or lose.

Mya didn't feel any better as the morning wore on. She thought maybe eating breakfast would make her stomachache go away, but it didn't. She wasn't very hungry, and she didn't eat much. Mya's heart was pounding. She knew she had to snap out of it if she was going to play well and score goals.

14

In the middle of a game, anxiety can prove to be a friend by helping to trigger the body's responses to a challenge.

When she arrived at the field, Mya felt even worse. People were starting to stream onto the bleachers, and a few seemed to be pointing at her. Mya imagined all those people watching her miss a winning goal. She had to stop herself from falling down right on the field in front of everyone.

Then, as the game started, Mya felt all her bad feelings slip away. She loved playing soccer, and now she could focus on running and kicking, not the crowd around her. She loved playing, so she turned her attention to the game, not the crowd.

The other team worried her a little, though. Most of the players were really fast, and several were very large—much bigger than her. They looked like they worked out a lot and were very serious about the game. This would be a hard team to beat. But fortunately, Mya was playing like her usual self. She hadn't scored any goals yet, but they had only been playing for a few minutes. At last, she found herself with the ball and a clear path to the goal. This was her chance!

She turned toward the goal. As she started to move toward it, she saw a player running toward her out of the corner of her eye. The other player was the biggest and fastest person on the team. She clearly worked out a lot, and she was ready to defend her team's goal no matter what. Suddenly, Mya was scared. She was used to dodging around smaller players who were trying to get the ball away from her. This player looked like she would knock Mya down if that's what it took to prevent her from scoring a goal.

For a second, Mya didn't know what to do. Time seemed to slow down a little, and it seemed like everything was happening in slow motion. She watched as the player ran toward her. Mya had time to imagine what would happen if the other player knocked into her. Bruises and broken bones came to mind. She even thought very briefly about running full tilt into the other player to try and knock her down first.

Instead, Mya sped up. She didn't want to get knocked down, and she wanted to make the goal, so she ran as fast as she could. She could feel the player right behind her, which just made her

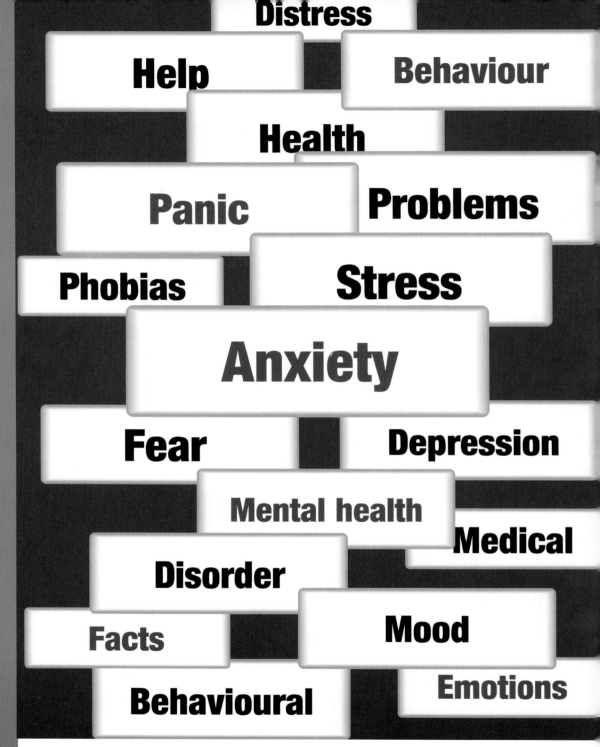

Anxiety occurs at many different levels. It may also involve other physical and emotional conditions.

## Make Connections

No one agrees on how many emotions there are. Over the years, different thinkers and scientists have come up with different lists of emotions. Here are some of the different types of emotions in each category of emotion. Humans have a lot of feelings!

- anger: rage, irritation, jealousy, dislike
- disgust: revulsion, contempt
- fear: alarm, shock, horror, terror, nervousness, worry
- hope: expectance, optimism
- joy: pride, contentment, cheerfulness, relief, excitement
- love: affection, attraction, infatuation
- sadness: despair, grief, disappointment, loneliness, guilt
- surprise: amazement, astonishment

run even faster. Then she kicked, watched the ball soar toward the goal . . . and go into the net! She had scored a goal for her team!

All the bad feelings Mya had before the game began had completely disappeared now!

## CONNECTED BUT DIFFERENT

The different emotions Mya felt on the day of her soccer game were connected but different. When she woke up, Mya felt anxious. Anxiety is uneasiness or **apprehension** about something that isn't right in front of you. Mya was anxious about the soccer game for days ahead of time, even though she wasn't yet playing in the game.

Anxiety is also an emotional response to something that does not really **threaten** your physical safety. Mya was not anxious about getting hurt in the soccer game when she was imagining it for days ahead of time. Mya was anxious that she wouldn't play well during her game, and that she wouldn't score any goals. She was anxious that other people would think she was a bad player and that she would embarrass herself in front of the crowd. Playing badly wouldn't have been a pleasant experience, but it wouldn't have been dangerous. Mya's health and safety would not have been threatened if she played badly.

Later, during the soccer game, Mya felt a different emotion called fear. She was afraid of the other player because she could have hurt Mya. Fear is apprehension based on something specific and **potentially** harmful—in this case, another soccer player knocking her down. People feel fear about threats to their safety. They may be afraid of fire, snakes, heights, or other things that can hurt them. Fear is directed toward something right in front of you. The larger soccer player was running right at Mya during the game, creating fear.

Both fear and anxiety are normal, human emotions. Small doses of them help people stay safe, healthy, and happy, although bigger doses can be unhealthy and get in the way of normal daily activities and happiness. Healthy amounts of fear and anxiety are just two of the many, many emotions we all have every day, all day.

The more you know about fear and anxiety, the better. You'll

## Text-Dependent Questions

1. Explain how this chapter defines anxiety.

2. Describe the feelings Mya had that indicate she was anxious.

3. How is fear different from anxiety, according to this chapter?

4. What was Mya afraid of?

start to understand why you feel the way you do and how to deal with your feelings when they start to get out of control. Figuring out your emotions is a big part of growing up!

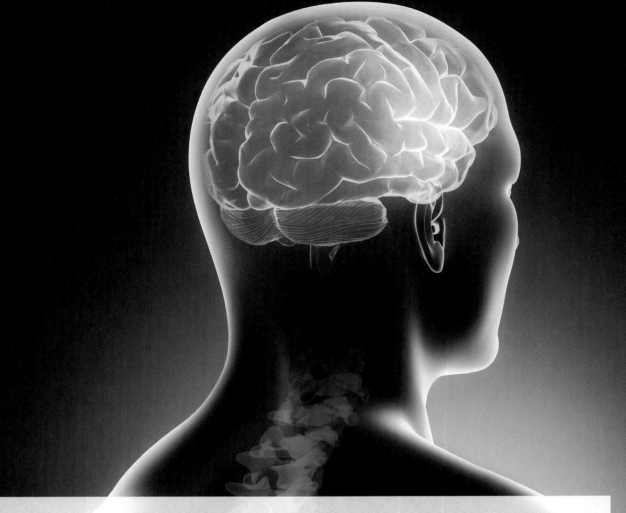

# Words to Understand

***researching:*** Studying a scientific question to try to learn more.

***depressed:*** Feeling unhappy or hopeless, often for a long time.

***stimulus:*** Something that triggers a response.

***automatic:*** Happening by itself, without being controlled by something or someone else.

# TWO

# WHAT HAPPENS TO YOU WHEN YOU FEEL FEAR AND ANXIETY?

Emotions don't just come from nowhere. Scientists have been *researching* the origins and causes of emotions for years. Their findings can give us important insights into why humans feel the emotions they do.

## EMOTIONAL SCIENCE

Emotions are all about the brain. People may feel the effects of emotions in the rest of the body (like Mya's stomachache, caused by her anxiety), but they come from the brain.

The brain is made up of billions of tiny cells called neurons. There are about 100 billion neurons in your brain, and even more in the rest of your body! The neurons in your brain are sending messages to each other all the time, which allows people to think, move, and sense things.

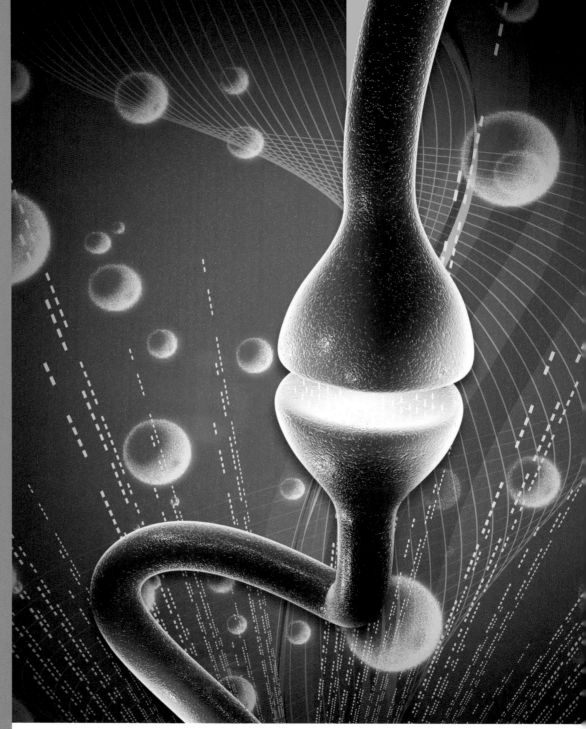

Neurons have branch-like parts called dendrites that reach out to the next neuron—but they never quite touch each other. Neurotransmitters carry signals across the tiny space between them.

Neurons use chemicals to send signals from one to the other, all over the body. Those chemicals actually turn into electricity, which cause other neurons to release chemicals, resulting in more electricity. The whole process happens over and over again, which is how messages get from your brain to the rest of your body.

Neurons are made up of three parts. The first part is the cell body, also called the soma. The soma is like the command center of the cell—it keeps the neuron going. Every neuron also has an axon, which is long and skinny. The axon carries electrochemical signals away from the soma and toward another neuron. Dendrites are the third part of a neuron. Dendrites look like tree branches. They receive electrochemical signals from other neurons and carry them to the soma.

Each neuron is isolated from all the others, which means no neurons touch each other. Yet neurons still send messages using electrochemical signals all over the body. Neurons obviously can't have conversations with each other using speech, so they communicate with each other in a different way. They use chemicals called neurotransmitters to carry messages across the tiny spaces between each other.

One neuron will send out a neurotransmitter, which will travel across the synapse, which is the gap between neurons. The chemicals are taken up by the dendrites of a second neuron nearby, and the message is sent on to the next neuron, and then the next, and the next.

Neurotransmitters are the key to emotions. There are dozens of kinds of neurotransmitters, and many are connected to familiar emotions like happiness and sadness. For example, the neurotransmitter serotonin has a lot to do with happiness and feelings of peacefulness. The correct balance of serotonin in your brain keeps you content and happy. Imbalances of serotonin, though, can lead to **depressed** moods. Of course, the science of emotions isn't quite as simple as that, since many neurotransmitters all work together to create emotions.

The process of feeling and interpreting emotions happens

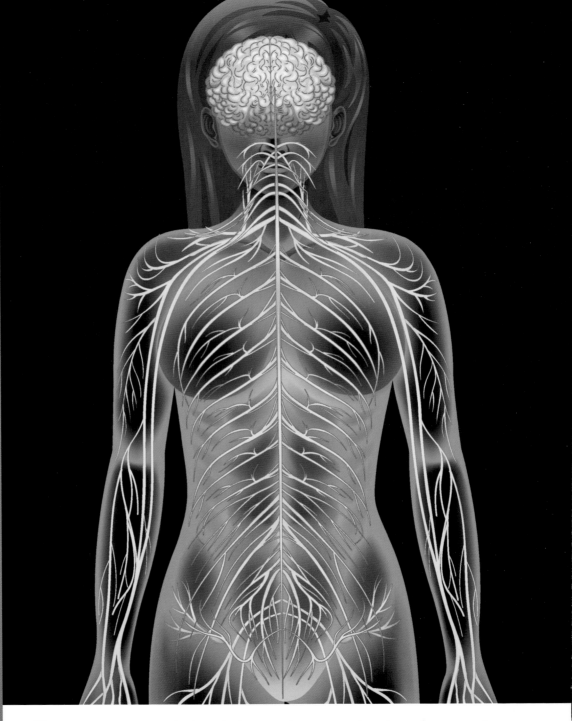

The nervous system, which includes your brain, reaches through your entire body.

## Make Connections

The brain isn't the only part of your body with neurons. Neurons are all over, including in your fingertips, spinal cord, stomach, and almost every other part of your body. The whole structure of neurons taken together is called the nervous system. Without a nervous system, you couldn't think, move, or even perform basic body functions like digestion and breathing.

mainly in the amygdala, a specific part of the brain. The brain has two almond-shaped amygdalae deep in the center. Each amygdala takes in what's happening in the environment—like a sad movie—and translates it into emotions like sadness. The amygdalae aren't the only parts of the brain involved in emotions, but they play a very important role.

## FIGHT-OR-FLIGHT

Everybody experiences fear at least once in a while, during every stage of life. Think back to when you were younger—what were you afraid of? Younger children are often afraid of the dark, strangers, being separated from family, monsters, dogs, thunderstorms, and fireworks.

Older people are afraid of some of these things too, but these kinds of fears are likely to weaken as people grow up. That doesn't mean teens and adults don't feel any fear. The kind of fear older people feel just tends to be a little different. People are often afraid of spiders and snakes, the doctor or dentist, natural disasters, failing, being rejected, getting hurt, and dying. Everyone's list of fears is different.

Fear is easily recognizable by the way it makes you feel. Although your brain is very much involved in fear, your body also

# FEAR AND ANXIETY

Why is it fun to watch a scary movie? Scientists have a couple of ideas—but what do YOU think?

## Make Connections

Roller coasters, scary movies, and haunted houses are all examples of fear people enjoy on a regular basis. But why do some people actually seek out fear? Scientists don't know for sure. Some researchers think people like the feeling of relief at the end, when we feel safe again. Others think people are really feeling excitement, not fear, when they do these things. And still others believe people actually enjoy the feeling of fear. When we seek out fear, we know we're not really in any danger. A scary movie isn't actually going to hurt you, so you can focus on the rush and excitement you feel from the fight-or-flight response, without worrying about something bad happening.

physically reacts to fear. Your heart beats faster. You sweat more, but your mouth becomes dry. Your legs might feel a little like jelly.

The body's reaction to fear is a scientific fact. The reaction is called the "fight-or-flight" response. When you encounter something scary or nerve wracking, your body goes into fight-or-flight mode. The changes that happen in your body get you ready to stay safe from the scary *stimulus* by either fighting back or running away (fleeing).

The process of feeling fear involves the environment, your brain, and the rest of your body. First, you must encounter and recognize a scary situation. You could be walking down a dark hallway without a light, taking off in an airplane for the first time, or watching a scary movie. You take in what's happening through your senses, like your eyes and ears. Your eyes and ears send what's going on in the world to your brain, and then your brain kicks into action.

Your brain processes the situation as something to be afraid of and then sends the signal to the rest of your body to go into fight-or-flight mode. The neurons in the amygdala and other parts

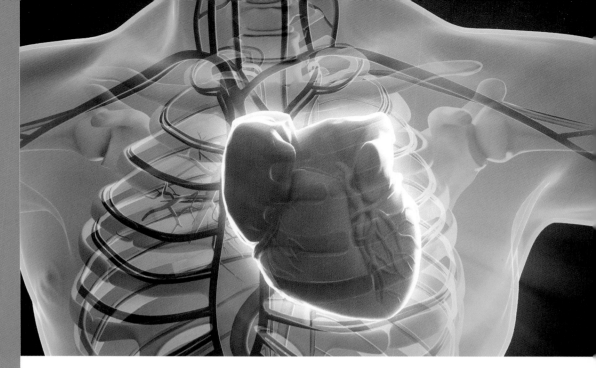

When you're scared your heart beats faster, sending more blood to your muscles, getting them ready to take action.

of the brain fire off neurotransmitters. The brain sends these signals to the body through the **automatic** nervous system. You don't have to make yourself go into the fight-or-flight mode. Your brain does it for you automatically.

Specific things happen in your body now. When you get scared, your lungs take in more air so your body has more oxygen, and you can either fight or flee. That's what's happening if you find yourself breathing faster and more deeply when you're afraid. Your heart pumps faster to get more blood to your muscles, making it easier to be strong and fight or run away fast. Your digestive system also slows down for a little while, which explains the dry mouth. The pupils in your eyes get bigger so you can see better. This is what people mean when they say, "His eyes got big."

The fight-or-flight response has helped humans survive for a long time. If people didn't feel fear in this way, they might put themselves in more danger. If someone being attacked by a wild animal just sat and stared at the attacker, the wild animal would probably finish her off pretty quickly! Instead, because she feels the fight-or-flight response, she is more likely to survive. She can face the animal and get ready to use all her strength to fight it off. Or she could run away as fast as she can. The choice she makes depends on the situation. If the wild animal in question were an angry bear, she would probably run away. If the animal were an angry but much smaller snake, she might choose to fight it off.

People today face different dangers from what people encountered thousands of years ago. Cars, guns, and airplanes are examples of relatively new things in the course of human history that people may fear. Luckily, the brain can react to new sources of fear. It still triggers the fight-or-flight mode.

## ANXIETY

Anxiety is a lot like fear, but people feel anxious when they aren't facing a specific threat that is right in front of them and that can hurt them. However, the body treats sources of anxiety similarly to sources of fear.

The body goes through the same fight-or-flight response with anxiety as it does with fear. The thought of starting the school year at a new school, for example, can cause anxiety. Your heart might beat faster on the first day, you might start breathing deeper and more quickly, and you might feel ready to run off at any second. That's the fight-or-flight response, even though you don't have anything specific to be afraid of. The first day of school isn't going to hurt you physically. You're just anticipating bad things happening.

You can use other words to describe anxiety, like nervousness, stress, uneasiness, and worry. Anxiety can be a mild feeling, or it can be really intense. If you're having trouble deciding whether you're anxious or afraid, think about whether or not what you're afraid of could really hurt you. You might feel threatened by having to give a speech because you might embarrass yourself, but

## Research Project

Using the Internet and the library, find out more about neurons and how they pass messages. Draw a diagram of a two neurons, labeling each part, including the synapse. Find the names of three or more neurotransmitters and use your diagram to show what they do.

even if you make a mistake, you won't get hurt. Plus, you're worrying about giving the speech before it happens. You're feeling anxious.

Anxiety affects your body too, just like fear. If you feel anxious about taking a test, your anxiety may start a couple days before the test and last until you're done taking the test. You can feel other emotions alongside anxiety, so during those couple days, you might also feel happy, angry, sad, frustrated, excited, and much more, but your anxiety is always in the background. During the time you're most anxious, you might have trouble concentrating and sleeping. You might feel your heart racing for days, and be a little jumpy about loud sounds or sudden movements. Most of the time, anxiety feels like fear, but sometimes a little less intense.

A little bit of anxiety can be helpful, but a lot of anxiety may interfere with your life. Anxiety has a lot of side effects for your body and mental state. Lots of anxiety can dull your appetite or make you eat more, make it hard to fall asleep and stay asleep, and keep you from concentrating.

Anxiety works a lot like fear. Neurotransmitters in your brain send messages to neurons in the rest of your body in response to a stimulus. Those messages tell the body to go into fight-or-flight mode.

Scientists have spent a lot of time studying what happens in the brains of people who feel too much anxiety. Many researchers

## Text-Dependent Questions

1. Describe what neurons do.

2. What is a synapse?

3. Explain what a neurotransmitter does.

4. According to this chapter, what role does the amygdala play in emotions?

5. Explain the fight-or-flight reaction.

think the neurotransmitter system that carries messages between neurons in the brain can have some trouble, and this is what causes problems with too much anxiety. For example, imbalances in the neurotransmitter GABA (gamma aminobutyric acid) seem to lead to problems with anxiety.

People with too much anxiety may have anxiety disorders. Anxiety disorders are mental health illnesses, which are actually quite common. Having a mental health problem doesn't make someone weird or bad—that person just needs some help to get back to normal.

Because fear and anxiety are unpleasant, and because too much of them can cause problems, we tend to think about fear and anxiety as negative emotions. They aren't feelings people like to have. There's a lot more to fear and anxiety, though. Both emotions can affect us in both positive and negative ways. As you learn more about fear and anxiety, you'll discover that even negative emotions can help you.

## Words to Understand

**sophisticated:** Complicated or advanced.
**moderate:** Medium or average.
**generalized:** Affecting everything; always there.

# THREE

## How Do Fear and Anxiety Affect Your Life?

Emotions have consequences. They make us react and change our environments or the way we think—either to keep the emotion going if it's pleasant, or to get rid of it if it's negative. Positive feelings of happiness, pleasure, and excitement usually mean you want to keep doing whatever is producing that feeling. Negative feelings tend to be warnings that make us change something so that we can feel better. The line between positive and negative feelings isn't clear cut, though. Even negative feelings are very useful. Fear and anxiety, for instance, are both very useful warnings. You should always pay attention to your fear and anxiety, to figure out how they can be useful to you!

Being scared of a stranger in a dark alley is a sensible response that may keep you safe.

# FEAR

Fear is actually a very useful emotion. Fear keeps you safe from all sorts of things, from strangers to fire. The fight-or-flight response isn't always pleasant, but it's a great warning.

Imagine you're walking down a dark alley alone, and you hear footsteps behind you. You're already kind of nervous being in the dark, but as soon as you hear those footsteps, your brain kicks into full fight-or-flight mode. Without even thinking, you start running home and make it inside without anything happening.

Now imagine you didn't feel that thrill of fear from the footsteps. Instead, you heard them but didn't react. You didn't really think much about them, even though you noticed they were getting faster. You don't run away. You might be putting yourself in danger. The person whose footsteps you're hearing might want to rob you or hurt you.

In situations like these, your fear keeps you safe. Feeling the fear wasn't very pleasant—but you probably would have rather felt the fear and stayed safe! Think of all the things fear keeps you safe from. Fear of fire keeps you from getting burned, fear of heights keeps you from climbing too high and falling, fear of a bully keeps you from getting beaten up. Sometimes fears don't always make sense, but in general, they keep you safe.

You may notice that your fears have changed over your lifetime. When you were younger, you might have been afraid of monsters. Now that you're older, you know monsters aren't real. It doesn't make sense to be afraid of them, so you no longer feel fear when you think about monsters. Your fear response system is more focused on things that can actually hurt you. As you grow up, your brain's warning system gets more *sophisticated*.

# ANXIETY

At first, anxiety seems pretty useless. Why would you want to feel nervous and apprehensive about something instead of confident and cool? But like fear, anxiety can actually be quite useful.

Shyness is a form of anxiety. Most everyone feels shy sometimes—but extreme shyness can be like a lock that prevents a person from interacting with others.

## Make Connections

Shyness is experiencing anxiety around other people. If you're shy, you may not feel comfortable talking to new people or people you don't know very well. You don't always want to talk in class. Lots of young people and adults are shy. Being shy isn't a bad thing—it's just the way some people are. If you just need some time to watch what's happening and get to know people a little better before you fully participate, that's okay. People who are severely shy, though, can have trouble making friends and doing things with others. Severe shyness is called social anxiety, and it gets in the way of a happy life much more than regular shyness does.

Anxiety gets you ready to face anything. A little bit of anxiety helps you face whatever you're anxious about, whether that's giving a report in class, having a difficult conversation with a friend, or starting a new school. The boost your brain gives you through the fight-or-flight mode helps you prepare. In chapter 1, Mya's anxiety about her soccer game probably helped her a little. She may have ran a little faster and controlled the ball better because her body was in fight-or-flight mode.

One study researchers did looked at how anxiety affected patients' recovery after surgery. The study compared patients who didn't have much anxiety before the surgery, patients who had *moderate* anxiety, and patients who had a lot of anxiety about surgery. The researchers found that the patients with moderate anxiety did the best after surgery. Patients with very little or a lot of anxiety did worse. The study suggests some anxiety helps you deal with stressful situations and makes you better off in the long run.

The fear of public speaking is very common. We often imagine the worst-case scenarios—but things are likely to go better than you imagine them! This is an example of a fear that's not very useful.

The fear of snakes is also very common. But are the snakes you run into outside of zoos actually dangerous?

## TOO MUCH

Small amounts of fear and anxiety are useful parts of normal life. Larger amounts, however, are not so helpful. Although fear can be helpful, it can also be unhealthy. Fear can keep people from doing things that aren't really that scary, or that they would actually enjoy if they weren't afraid. Someone who is afraid of everything will never try new things.

The next time you're afraid of something, stop and think about it. Ask yourself if it makes sense to be afraid. Take snakes, for example. Lots of people are afraid of snakes. Scientists even think that our brains are hardwired to be afraid of snakes. In one way, being afraid of snakes does make sense. Some snakes are venomous and can kill you or make you sick. The fight-or-flight mode is very useful if you're likely to be running into a venomous snake. However, many people live in places where snakes aren't

Lots of people are scared of spiders. It's only a phobia when the fear becomes so extreme that the person starts arranging his whole life around avoiding spiders.

## Make Connections

Phobias often seem amusing, since they're triggered by what you might think are normal, everyday things. For the people with the phobias, though, their fears make their lives really hard! Here's a list of some of the more unusual phobias:

- kathisophobia: the fear of sitting down
- octophobia: the fear of the number eight
- dendrophobia: the fear of trees
- paraskavedekatriaphobia: the fear of Friday the 13th
- xanthophobia: the fear of the color yellow
- metrophobia: the fear of poetry
- omphalophobia: the fear of belly buttons
- phobophobia: the fear of fear

venomous. The snakes that live in the area are harmless and don't hurt people. The fear response to snakes doesn't make as much sense anymore.

Really extreme fears and anxieties are also not healthy. Fear and anxiety should be temporary emotions you experience every once in a while. If you are feeling them all the time, or feeling them very intensely, your fear and anxiety may be a problem.

Some people experience extreme fears called phobias. Phobias are when fear gets out of control. People with phobias are extremely fearful of one particular thing, like spiders or heights. Common phobias include trypanophobia (the fear of flying), arachnophobia (the fear of spiders), and acrophobia (the fear of heights). There are dozens of phobias out there.

People can live with phobias, although these fears can make life harder. Someone who is afraid of heights might not want to

# FEAR AND ANXIETY

The fear of heights can be normal and healthy. It's sensible not to take risks in situations where you could fall and hurt yourself. A person with a phobia about heights, however, might find herself unable to go into tall buildings or enjoy a picnic on a hillside.

hike up to a mountaintop or take an elevator to the top floor of a building. Her height phobia might not be a big deal. But what if this person had a chance for job with a company that turned out to be on the top floor of a tall building? The job is one she's always wanted—but her fear of heights won't let her even go to the interview. Now her phobia is getting in the way of her life.

Phobias have a way of doing that. Someone with arachnophobia, for example, doesn't just get scared if there happens to be a spider crawling on him. Instead, his body might go into fight-or-flight mode when he even sees a picture of a spider, reads about a spider, or maybe just thinks about spiders. He may not even be able to go outside if he has severe arachnophobia, for fear of encountering a spider.

Other phobias make life even harder. A person who has a phobia of darkness (called nyctophobia) will encounter lots of difficulties. She'll have to face her phobia every night, and she may take extreme measures to avoid the dark. Maybe she'll sleep with the lights on at night. She won't go out at night to hang out with friends and family, or to do other things she may want to do. If she happens to live somewhere that gets dark very early in the winter, her life is even harder. Clearly, her phobia is fear gone too far.

People can develop phobias at any time during their lives. Sometimes phobias are triggered by a particular event. If a dog bit you, you might suddenly develop a phobia about dogs. One bad experience with a dog makes all dogs scary. Other people develop phobias without any particular event happening. And some people are just naturally more sensitive to fear and phobias than others.

Too much anxiety is just as bad as too much fear. Even though a little anxiety can help you perform better on a test, a speech, or a tryout, a lot of anxiety is damaging. High levels of anxiety make performing well harder. The fight-or-flight response only helps to a certain point. In the anxiety study cited above, the patients with a lot of anxiety did worse during their recovery from surgery than patients with moderate anxiety.

Too much fear and anxiety aren't good for us—but it's often hard to get control of our fears. We may need help from a professional in that case.

## Make Connections

Psychologists are studying what they call anxiety sensitivity—anxiety about feeling anxiety. People who have anxiety sensitivity worry about showing their anxiety to other people. They think terrible things will happen if they get too anxious. That just leads to even more anxiety! Psychologists have found that people with anxiety sensitivity are more likely to be depressed too. Researchers are doing more studies to find out just how strong that link is, and how to help people who are sensitive to anxiety.

Anxiety disorders are the most extreme form of anxiety. People with anxiety disorders have a lot of worry, nervousness, and dread. Anxiety isn't just something they feel once in a while, like before a test or an audition. They live with anxiety all the time. Too much anxiety doesn't leave room for other emotions and experiences. If anxiety is keeping you from doing things you want to do too often, your anxiety may be unhealthy.

There are several different kinds of anxiety disorders. One is *generalized* anxiety, when someone is anxious about many different things, like school, friends, family, and the future. He never gets much of a break from his anxiety because he's anxious about *everything*. Another kind of anxiety disorder is social anxiety, when a person gets intensely nervous in front of other people and often can't be around others for long. Social anxiety makes school, work, and a social life very hard. Post-traumatic stress disorder (PTSD) is yet another kind of anxiety disorder. People develop PTSD after something awful happens, like a car crash, going to war, or being the victim of a violent crime. PTSD makes people relive the event over and over again, along with their anxiety.

## Research Project

One of the sidebars in this chapter lists the names of several different kinds of phobias. Use a dictionary that provides words' root meanings to discover what language these different phobias' names come from. Then use the Internet or the library to discover whether people actually suffer from these phobias, and if so, how common they are. See if you can discover the names of other unusual phobias as well.

Anxiety disorders make everyday things hard. Going to sleep and getting a good night's rest is hard. Eating the right amount of food is hard, since many anxious people either have no appetite or eat too much. Just relaxing is hard if the person's heart is always pounding. Being anxious all the time is tiring!

Anxiety disorders also affect people mentally. Someone with an anxiety disorder may not have a lot of self-confidence. She may feel bad she's anxious all the time and think she's not a valuable person. Anxiety also gets in the way of concentrating and being involved in things in school and at home. If you're anxious all day, you'll find it hard to pay attention to the teacher and do your homework. Plus, people with anxiety disorders often feel alone. If they don't know anyone else with an anxiety disorder, they may feel like no one understands them. They seem like the only ones who have this problem. That's just not true, of course—lots and lots of people suffer from anxiety disorders. The National Institute of Mental Health estimates 40 million people have an anxiety disorder in the United States alone.

Anxiety also goes hand-in-hand with depression. Depression is a long-lasting, serious feeling of sadness and hopelessness. People with depression don't enjoy doing the things they used to

## Text-Dependent Questions

1. Explain how fear can be a useful emotion.

2. How have researchers found that anxiety can help us?

3. Explain how shyness and anxiety are related.

4. Describe how phobias can interfere with daily life. What examples are given in this chapter?

5. List three kinds of anxiety disorders and explain what each is.

do. They are often withdrawn from friends and family, and they find day-to-day living more difficult than most people.

Fortunately, there's a lot of help available for people who suffer from fear and anxiety. And there's a lot to learn from fear and anxiety too! Learning from your emotions makes them less scary, and helps you live a happier, healthier emotional life.

# Words to Understand

**psychologists:** Experts in the mind and emotions.
**demonstrative:** Tending to show feelings openly.
**productive:** Getting things done or having a good result.
**destructive:** Hurting people or undoing past progress.
**realistic:** Sensible and practical; having to do with something that could actually happen.

# FOUR

## Learning from Your Emotions

Some people think negative feelings like fear and anxiety are just plain unpleasant. You can't avoid emotions, though. Positive and negative feelings are both part of everyone's lives. **Psychologists**, researchers, and everyday people have learned that people are much better off if they learn to accept emotions and learn from them.

As young people grow up, they usually learn to identify emotions better and better. With practice, people are able to listen to what their emotions are telling them. Another important part of growing up is learning to decide when emotions are healthy and when they are too much. Figuring out your emotions isn't always easy, but you'll have a healthier, happier life if you do!

## ACCEPTING EMOTIONS

To learn from emotions, people first have to accept them. Accepting emotions isn't always as easy as it sounds, and a lot of people struggle with it. Accepting emotions means allowing yourself to feel everything you feel, even unpleasant emotions like fear and anxiety.

Everyone handles emotions differently. Some people just want to be alone when they're dealing with intense feelings. This is okay up to a point—but if a person shuts herself off from others for too long because of her emotions, she may need help from her friends, family, or professionals.

Many people fight their emotions or ignore them. They don't want to feel badly, so they push their feelings away or pretend they don't exist. Unfortunately, that doesn't work. When people try to ignore their emotions, they're still in there, and they're still affecting the brain and body. Because we're humans, we can't get away from emotions. Learning to accept emotions makes life a lot better in the long run, even if we have to feel some unpleasant things sometimes.

For instance, people often push their sadness away after someone close to them dies. Let's say your friend's grandfather died. Most people are really sad when a grandparent dies. Your friend doesn't seem very upset though, even though you know he loved his grandfather and spent a lot of time with him. You expect him to show at least some sadness.

What's going on? Why isn't he crying or telling you how sad he is? Instead, he's just going through his days like nothing happened. He may just be someone who is not very **demonstrative** with his emotions, even though he's feeling them inside. You can't really tell unless you talk to him. But he may also be pushing his emotions away instead of accepting them and letting himself feel sad. Instead of thinking about his grandfather and grieving, he's pretending like the death doesn't affect him. Ignoring sadness may seem like a good solution—why feel bad if you don't have to? But your friend hasn't really gotten rid of the sadness.

Instead, the sadness will come out in other ways later on. Buried emotions can lead to physical illness, depression, anger, violence, drug use, and poor relationships with others. Your friend can avoid some of these negative consequences by just letting himself feel sad for a while.

## BE THE BOSS

Accepting emotions doesn't mean that you just have to be at their mercy all the time. You can be the boss of emotions while still accepting that you have them.

Feeling angry with their parents is pretty common for teenagers. Learning to handle your anger in positive ways is a big step toward being in control of your emotions.

Being the boss of your emotions means choosing how you respond to them. People can choose to respond to emotions in healthy, *productive* ways or unhealthy, *destructive* ways. Once you know you have that choice, you can accept your emotions but also keep control over them.

Maybe you have another friend who has problems with anger. She gets angry pretty easily, and she lets her anger show itself in unhealthy ways. The last time she got angry was because you refused to let her borrow a video game. You weren't sure she'd give it back, and you had saved up a lot of money to buy that game. You invited her over to your house to play it instead, but she just got mad because she wanted to take it home with her. She yelled at you in front of all your friends, and then she started spreading rumors about you.

Clearly, your friend didn't express her anger in a very healthy way. Yelling in a public place and spreading rumors is not the best way to respond to anger. Plus, you're not sure how much more you can take before you decide not to be friends anymore, so she's close to losing a friend too.

Your friend has other options, though. She can't necessarily stop herself from feeling angry about things. Feeling angry is normal, and some people get angry more than others. However, she doesn't have to yell and spread rumors. She can choose to step back from the situation and calm down first. She can take out her anger by running or doing some other strenuous exercise. She could write down her feelings in a journal. She could yell into a pillow instead of at other people. How she expresses her anger is up to her! She can be the boss.

Being the boss of your emotions is hard work. It isn't easy for most people. Once you know that you can choose how to express your emotions, you have to decide how to express them. Choosing how to express emotions in a healthy way is a learning process. Then comes practice. People may not always be able to control their emotions at first, but with practice they tend to get better.

Taking deep breaths often works, no matter what the emotion is. Expressing emotions with writing, art, or physical activity works

Remind yourself that you control your emotions—you don't have to let them control you.

for many people. Talking about feelings with friends, family, or a therapist is usually helpful. Different things work for different people.

Choosing how to respond to emotion doesn't mean never showing emotion. It just means showing emotions in ways that don't hurt other people or yourself. To go back to your friend whose grandfather died, it's totally okay if he cries in front of people. Crying is a normal sign of sadness. Talking about his sadness, not smiling a lot, and not wanting to join in activities he normally enjoys for a little while is also normal.

## LISTENING TO YOUR FEARS AND ANXIETIES

As with other emotions, listening to fear and anxiety helps people learn from them. Remember, the main purpose of fear and anxiety is to keep you safe. A lot of the time, people can keep themselves out of trouble if they just listen to their fear and anxiety. Fears and anxieties are telling you something—don't ignore them!

## Make Connections

 Talking about emotions is one of the healthiest ways of dealing with them. Talk to a close friend, a family member, or someone trained to help you with emotions and problems, like a guidance counselor, psychologist, or social worker. Talking about emotions helps you sort out how you feel, and may even help you figure out ways to deal with your emotions or the situations that are causing them. Talking may lead you to change something in your environment or start thinking about a situation differently so that you can feel better. Talking makes you feel like you have support, so you don't feel so alone. People find that talking about difficult emotions is a big relief, and those same emotions aren't so much of a problem after talking.

Fears and anxieties give us really useful messages. Fear of snowboarding, for example, makes sense—people can get hurt really badly by sliding down a mountain on a board. In this case, fear of snowboarding doesn't have to mean you never snowboard. It does mean the fear should make you cautious when you snowboard. The first time you snowboard, you're probably too afraid to start on the hardest slopes. You're smart if you listen to that fear and learn from it, because you'll keep yourself safe by staying on the smaller, easier slopes and working your way up as your snowboarding skills grow. Fears and anxieties don't have to make you avoid activities or situations—just to be careful about them.

Learning from fear and anxiety isn't always easy. Sometimes the messages that fear and anxiety are telling us are buried deep and take some thinking and exploring. If you're anxious all the time about crossing everything off on your to-do list, your anxiety is telling you something. What it's telling you is not obvious, though—not like your fear of an angry bear growling at you,

If you feel stressed out and anxious because there just doesn't seem to be enough time in the day to do all your homework, your emotions could be telling you something important about your life.

which is clearly telling you to run away! Your anxiety may be telling you you're doing too much and that you need to relax. Anxiety is indicating you need to change something. The right way to listen to and learn from your anxiety in this case would be to make your to-do list shorter and see if your anxiety still bothers you. In addition, by paying attention to what you're afraid of or anxious about, you'll learn more about yourself. With your to-do list, you might realize that you feel like you have to be productive all the time and do everything perfectly. Your anxiety is telling you something about the way you think. Maybe you want to consider trying to change.

Fear and anxiety tell us something isn't right. They tell us that something needs to change, either in our environment or in the way we think. Anxiety about a to-do list sends the message that the environment (the number of things on your to-do list) needs to be different. It also tells you the way you're thinking (the need to do everything perfectly) isn't working for you very well.

## CONQUERING YOUR FEARS AND ANXIETIES

One trick to learning from your fears and anxieties is telling the difference between when they are *realistic* and when they are getting in the way. For example, imagine you're afraid of dogs. Maybe a dog bit you when you were younger. Being afraid of dogs makes sense, because you've seen that dogs can be dangerous. But now you're so afraid of dogs that you won't go over to a friend's house if there's a dog there. Walking outside is even a little stressful whenever you see someone walking a dog.

So even though your fear of dogs is based in reality, it's not actually helping you. Most dogs are friendly and wouldn't bite you. There's no need to be afraid of every dog you see. In this case, you might want to rethink your fear and try to be a little less afraid around dogs. There's nothing wrong with caution, especially around more aggressive dogs, but many dogs are friendly.

Even people with extreme phobias can overcome fears that get in the way of life. The usual process, guided by a therapist,

## Research Project

The chapter mentions that therapists may use a process called gradual exposure to help people overcome phobias. Use the Internet or the library to find a case study of someone who went through gradual exposure. A case study is a report of a real-life situation, often written by a psychologist or a researcher. In your own words, write your own case study. Describe what the person was afraid of and how that fear affected the individual's life. Then list the steps the person went through during the process of gradual exposure. In the end, was the person able to overcome the phobia?

is called gradual exposure. This means the therapist exposes the person with the phobia to the object of fear in small steps. A therapist may first get someone with a dog phobia to just think about dogs. Then the patient will look at pictures of dog or watch a movie with a dog in it. Then she'll hold a stuffed dog and so on until she can be in the same room as a real dog. The theory is that each step of exposure isn't too stressful, but they all add up to real progress. The therapist may also work with the patient to change how she thinks and to find out the root of her fear of dogs.

Overcoming fears and anxieties isn't limited to people with phobias or anxiety disorders. You can conquer even everyday fears and anxieties just by dealing with them head on. Facing fears and anxieties is hard, but worthwhile!

When you face what you're afraid or anxious about (as long as you are truly safe doing so), you'll come to realize your fears and anxieties aren't realistic. If you're just mildly afraid of dogs, you may think that every dog will bite you. Plenty of dogs are friendly, though, and will not bite you. Once you start to be around friendly dogs, your thinking will change. You may now think that

## Text-Dependent Questions

1. What does this chapter indicate is the first step toward learning from your emotions?

2. Explain why ignoring or burying our emotions is not a good option.

3. The chapter indicates that we can respond to emotions either negatively or positively. What examples does the chapter give of someone responding negatively or destructively to emotions?

4. Describe healthy ways to respond to our emotions, according to this chapter.

5. What example does this chapter give of a fear that started out based in reality but became unrealistic and unhealthy?

only some dogs will bite you, and you'll see that you can tell the difference between aggressive and friendly dogs. Conquering your fear of dogs will take time, but it's possible!

Learning from fear and anxiety is a balancing act. On the one hand, paying attention to fears and anxieties keep us safe. These emotions are very useful tools to figure out how to stay out of danger. On the other hand, they tell us when we need to change our thinking patterns.

Understanding our emotions is a lifelong job. It's always challenging—but with practice, it gets easier!

# Find Out More

## IN BOOKS

Crist, James. *What to Do When You're Scared and Worried: A Guide for Kids.* Minneapolis, Minn.: Free Spirit Publishing, 2004.

Gallo, Donald R. *What Are You Afraid Of? Stories About Phobias.* Somerville, Mass.: Candlewick Press, 2006.

Levy, Joel. *Phobiapedia.* New York: Scholastic, 2011.

Tompkins, Michael A. and Katherine A. Martinez. *My Anxious Mind: A Teen's Guide to Managing Anxiety and Panic.* Washington, D.C.: Magination Press, 2010.

Wells, Polly. *Freaking Out: Real-life Stories About Anxiety.* Toronto, Ont.: Annick Press, 2013.

## ONLINE

KidsHealth: Being Afraid
kidshealth.org/kid/feeling/emotion/afraid.html

PBSKids.org: Emotions
pbskids.org/itsmylife/emotions/index.html

Psychologytoday.com
www.psychologytoday.com

TeensHealth: Anxiety Disorders
kidshealth.org/teen/your_mind/mental_health/anxiety.html

TeensHealth: Fears and Phobias
kidshealth.org/teen/cancer_center/feelings/phobias.html

# Series Glossary of Key Terms

**adrenaline:** An important body chemical that helps prepare your body for danger. Too much adrenaline can also cause stress and anxiety.

**amygdala:** An almond-shaped area within the brain where the flight-or-flight response takes place.

**autonomic nervous system:** The part of your nervous system that works without your conscious control, regulating body functions such as heartbeat, breathing, and digestion.

**cognitive:** Having to do with thinking and conscious mental activities.

**cortex:** The area of your brain where rational thinking takes place.

**dopamine:** A brain chemical that gives pleasure as a reward for certain activities.

**endorphins:** Brain chemicals that create feelings of happiness.

**fight-or-flight response:** Your brain's reaction to danger, which sends out messages to the rest of the body, getting it ready to either run away or fight.

**hippocampus:** Part of the brain's limbic system that plays an important role in memory.

**hypothalamus:** The brain structure that gets messages out to your body's autonomic nervous system, preparing it to face danger.

**limbic system:** The part of the brain where emotions are processed.

**neurons:** Nerve cells found in the brain, spinal cord, and throughout the body.

**neurotransmitters:** Chemicals that carry messages across the tiny gaps between nerve cells.

**serotonin:** A neurotransmitter that plays a role in happiness and depression.

**stress:** This feeling that life is just too much to handle can be triggered by anything that poses a threat to our well-being, including emotions, external events, and physical illnesses.

# Index

# About the Author & Consultant

Kim Etingoff lives in Boston, Massachusetts. She has written many books for young adults on a variety of topics related to healthy development.

Cindy Croft is director of the Center for Inclusive Child Care at Concordia University, St. Paul, Minnesota where she also serves as faculty in the College of Education. She is field faculty at the University of Minnesota Center for Early Education and Development program and teaches for the Minnesota on-line Eager To Learn program. She has her M.A. in education with early childhood emphasis. She has authored *The Six Keys: Strategies for Promoting Children's Mental Health in Early Childhood Programs* and co-authored *Children and Challenging Behavior: Making Inclusion Work* with Deborah Hewitt. She has worked in the early childhood field for the past twenty years.

# Picture Credits